Thomas Picton

Acrostics from Across the Atlantic

And Other Poems

Thomas Picton

Acrostics from Across the Atlantic
And Other Poems

ISBN/EAN: 9783744685788

Printed in Europe, USA, Canada, Australia, Japan

Cover: Foto ©Thomas Meinert / pixelio.de

More available books at **www.hansebooks.com**

ACROSTICS FROM ACROSS THE ATLANTIC

AND OTHER POEMS HUMOROUS

AND SENTIMENTAL

BY

A GOTHAMITE.

LONDON:

STEVENS BROTHERS, 17, HENRIETTA STREET,

COVENT GARDEN.

1869.

CONTENTS.

	Page
LINES written under George Fox's Oak at Flushing, Long Island	1
To Miss * * *, who sprained her foot on the first day of Lent	10
From "I Lombardi"	11
The West-End of London in September	14
The Naiad	18
Extract from a Letter to Mrs. * * *, of St. Louis	24
Acrostic addressed to Signorina Clotilde Barili	28
The Great Race between Fashion and Peytona	30
A Valentine sent to Miss * * *	35
Coralie. A Sketch	41
An Acrostic to a Young Lady of Philadelphia	47

CONTENTS.

	Page
Lines on the Fancy Ball, given at the Ocean House in Newport, Rhode Island	48
Lines written on the News reaching England that the State of California had adopted a Constitution prohibiting Slavery in her territory	54
Lines addressed to Miss * * *, of Katonah, New York	59

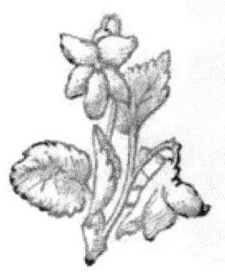

THE Author has been emboldened, by what he fears may be the undue partiality of friends, to present to the public this little unpretending volume of effusions; a few only of his youthful imagination, but all which have been preserved among the odds and ends of bygone days.

LINES WRITTEN UNDER GEORGE FOX'S OAK AT FLUSHING, LONG ISLAND,

BENEATH WHOSE SHADE THAT FAMOUS APOSTLE OF THE QUAKERS PREACHED DURING HIS VISIT IN 1672.

THERE'S many a spot that's dear to me on old Long Island's shore,
And hallow'd by the memories of a noble race of yore,
Who fled from England's tyranny or Puritanic sway,
When cruel laws, or bigot zeal, had driven them away.

But Flushing most of all I love, famed for its fruits
    and flowers,[1]
Where Pan roams free, if yet he roams, and Flora
    builds her bowers;
For my forefathers, when they reach'd these shores,
    did here abide,
Here pitch'd their tents, here rear'd their homes,
    and call'd the place Bayside.
No voice then 'mid the forest gloom, no footstep
    echo'd near,
Save when the tawny Indian pass'd and chased the
    flying deer.
The wielded axe had never made these lofty woods
    resound,
Nor patient ox, with guided plough, upturn'd the
    fruitful ground;

---

[1] Flushing is celebrated for its horticultural gardens and nurseries.

Now gardens, blooming all around, with perfume
    fill the air;
The reddest rose at Flushing grows, the fairest lily
    there.

Beneath this oak, where I now lie, George Fox, the
    Quaker, stood,
And preach'd, as John the Baptist preach'd, be-
    neath the spreading wood.
For persecution sought to drive his followers from
    the land,
And here, around him, came by stealth a little
    Christian band;
And one[1] of these, for conscience' sake, (whose
    blood flows in my veins,)

---

[1] John Bowne, who was arrested by Stuyvesant, Governor of New Amsterdam for entertaining Quakers, and having meetings of that Society at his house, and after being confined for three months at Fort Amsterdam, sent to Holland a

To Holland, prisoner, was sent, weigh'd down by
    heavy chains.

Imagination sways me now, dim fancies crowd my
    mind,
As underneath this old oak's shade I lie at length
    reclined ;
I hear George Fox with earnest voice pour forth
    the words of peace,
And pray the Lord that war and strife throughout
    the world may cease.
From Newtown kills,[1] from Hempstead plains, from
    Gravesend far away,

---

prisoner. He was released on his arrival there, by the Government of the Dutch West India Company, who reprimanded their officer for this act of tyranny. (*Vide* Thompson's "Long Island.")

[1] A word derived from the Dutch, signifying a stream or arm of the sea.

And from the wood-crown'd hills which skirt the shores of Oyster Bay;
Beneath the spreading canopy his followers draw near,
With holy zeal they forward press, the word of God to hear;
And save the breeze amid the trees no other sound is heard,
Unless, perchance, the melody of some wild forest bird.
The savage Indian stops anear, against a tree he stands,
He hears the messenger of peace, the bow drops from his hands.
'Tis past; George Fox, his followers, the Indian, all are gone,
And I beneath this old oak's shade am lying, all alone.

I've seen old England's oak, where once the Royal
    Martyr laid
And heard the Covenanter's words, while passing
    'neath its shade,
And dearer still, that other tree[1] in my own native
    land,
Where once the charter lay conceal'd, safe from a
    king's command.
But this old oak, which o'er me spreads and flings
    its shade around,
Is sanctified, and I now lie on consecrated ground.
A church it stands, whose pavement is the turf on
    which I tread,

---

[1] The charter granted by Charles II. to Connecticut Colony was annulled by James II. in 1686. Sir Edmund Andros, who had been recently appointed Governor of New England, repaired to Hartford, with a body of troops and demanded the surrender of the document, which being secretly conveyed to the hollow of an oak tree in the town, since known as the "Charter Oak," was there safely preserved.

Its trunk an altar, and for arch the branches overhead.
No splendid dome, though blest by priest, where thousands bend the knee
To worship God, is fitter place or holier than this tree.

A thousand years mayst thou, old oak, still flourish in the land,
Thy boughs still wave above, below, thy trunk still firmly stand.
Long ere the woodman's axe shall ring upon thy timbers staunch;
Long ere the robin cease to sing upon thy topmost branch;
Long ere the scathing lightning strike and rend thy limbs apart;
Long ere the gnawing worm shall come and penetrate thy heart;

Long may the birds build nests in thee, with oak
    twigs interlaid;
Long may young lovers breathe their vows beneath
    thy grateful shade;
Long may the cherished name be carved upon thy
    roughen'd bark;
Long mayst thou hear, above thee poised, at early
    dawn the lark;
Long ere the mellow earth refuse the sap unto thy
    roots;
Long may thy ripen'd acorns fall and rise again in
    shoots,
Which water'd by the showers above and nourished
    by the ground,
Shall grow till they become large oaks, and hemming
    thee around,
Protect their parent from rude blasts with more than
    filial love,
Until thou find'st thyself at last the patriarch of a
    grove.

But if thou too, like other trees, must share the fate
　　of all,
And should in future years arrive the day when thou
　　must fall,
No mansion may thy timbers form, nor yet upon
　　the seas,
In wandering ships be toss'd about at mercy of the
　　breeze ;
But, carved in many a quaint device, as long as oak
　　can last
Be treasured up and handed down as relics of the
　　past.

TO MISS * * *,

WHO SPRAINED HER FOOT ON THE FIRST DAY OF LENT.

TERPSICHORE, the charming maid
    To whom these lines are sent,
  Has sprain'd her foot, and I'm afraid
'Twas done because 'tis Lent.

For this dear girl, though Lent begin,
    From dancing can't abstain;
And so, to save her *soul* from sin,
    Her foot received a sprain.

FROM "I LOMBARDI."

EVERY frequenter of the Italian Opera in England or the States who is not familiar with the original, must have found the wretched English translation in the librettos a serious drawback to his enjoyment. The following lines are an attempt to render a part of the opera of " I Lombardi " into less objectionable language. If the translation has no other merit, it is, at any rate, literal.[1]

The Crusaders are besieging Antioch; Giselda, daughter of Arvino, the Christian leader, is a prisoner there with the Infidels. During her captivity a passion has sprung up between her and Oronte, son of Acciano, king of that city. At the assault and capture of the town by the Crusaders this monarch is slain by Giselda's father, and Oronte, wounded by the same hand, is left for dead on the field of battle. Arvino, at the head of the assailants, rushes into his daughter's presence, his

---

[1] The author has seen a libretto, published in London, differing somewhat from the Italian version he used.

FROM "I LOMBARDI."

sword stained with the blood of her lover and his father. She hears the well-known battle-cry of the Crusaders, "Dio lo vuole," "Dio lo vuole" (God wills it), and exclaims:

UNRIGHTEOUS cause, 'tis not of God,
Blood, human blood, now stains the sod;
Not holy zeal, but frenzy base,
Roused by the gold of Mah'met's race;
No words from heaven e'er bid us kill,
'Tis not God's will—'tis not God's will.

The dark veil falls before my eyes,
Oh, force divine! the conquer'd rise
With vengeance dire; such is the doom
Now hidden in the future's gloom;
To none was e'er the right bequeathed
To convert souls, where first they breathed,
The sacrifice of brothers slain
The God of life will sure disdain.

FROM "I LOMBARDI."

Sport of the winds, before my eyes
I see barbarian hordes arise;
The torrent sweeps o'er Europe's plains,
To bind her sons in servile chains.
God never made commands like these,
Ne'er bid us shed man's blood in seas,
Peace, peace alone, His words instil,
'Tis not God's will—'tis not God's will!

THE WEST-END OF LONDON IN SEPTEMBER.

OT a coach is heard
In thy bounds, Mayfair,
Not a knocker's stirr'd
Through Belgravia's square;
Not a horse is seen
In all Rotten Row,
And the grass grows green
Where it shouldn't grow.

Wandering up and down,
Not a soul I meet,

Save Policeman Brown,
Pacing on his beat;
Overwhelm'd with grief,
For he cannot spy
One kind cook with beef
Or mutton " on the sly."

Not a bright-eyed maid
Passes me with blushes,
Not a footman staid
In red or yellow plushes;
I see no powder'd head
Peering through the pane;
Is everybody dead
By pestilence, or slain?

No, my friends, but here,
Where fashion reigns supreme,
At this time of year
One must not be seen.

Some have gone to Cowes,
For the children's *weal;*
Some are bagging grouse,
And some have *cut* for Deal.

Some take rod for Wales,
While some prefer the Seine,
Some dive down Dove's deep dales,
Then—scramble back again;
Sandwich some may try,
Though oft'ner hot than cool,
And those who find Ham dry,
May start perchance for Pool.

Here am I forlorn,
Like another Crusoe,
All the world has gone
And I mean to do so.

LONDON IN SEPTEMBER.

Seek you solitude,
Then my words remember,
Try no desert rude,
But London in September.

THE NAIAD.

(TRANSLATED FROM THE RUSSIAN OF PUSHKIN.[1])

BY a forest-hidden lake,
    In a cabin rude,
  Dwelt a holy monk, who sought
Rest and solitude.

Here his daily life was pass'd,
    Many a rolling year,
In fasting, penitence, and prayer,
    And practices austere.

---

[1] Alexander Pushkin or Pouschkin, the most celebrated poet of Russia, who has often been compared to Byron, was born at St. Petersburgh, May 26, 1799; and died February 10, 1837.

THE NAIAD.

Digging in his narrow grave
    Was his daily task;
No wish had he, and when he pray'd,
    Only death to ask.

One day at the open door
    Knelt the anchorite,
While the forest darker grew
    With the shades of night.

From the waters of the lake
    Slowly mists arise,
Through the clouds the moon is seen
    Floating in the skies.

From his knees the hermit rose,
    Towards the lake he gazed,
Starts, and, with bewilder'd look,
    Stands like one amazed.

THE NAIAD.

The waters foam, then sink to rest,
 Then they foam again;
When suddenly a female form
 Rises from the main.

Light as shadows of the night,
 And white as morning snows
Upon the hills, the beauteous nymph
 From the lake arose.

Silently she draws anear,
 And sits upon the bank,
Gazing towards him, while she dries
 Her tresses moist and dank.

Moved, he contemplates her form,
 Tremblingly he stands,
Whilst the Naiad of the Lake
 Beckons with her hands.

THE NAIAD.

Then, like a shooting star whose track
　　We mark across the skies,
She sinks beneath the slumbering waves
　　Before his wondering eyes.

That night the aged hermit lay
　　Upon a sleepless bed,
And when the morning dawn'd, he rose,
　　His daily prayers unsaid.

Unwittingly before his eyes,
　　Whichever course they take,
Stands the shadowy figure of
　　The Naiad of the Lake.

Again the darkness of the night
　　The gloomy wood enshrouds,
Once more the pale and silvery moon
　　Mounts above the clouds.

The nymph arises from the lake
    With fair and lovely face,
Her arms outstretch'd towards the monk,
    Inviting to embrace.

Then playing with the sparkling waves,
    She child-like laughs and cries,
And calls the hermit to draw near,
    Between her tender sighs.

" Oh, hermit! hermit! hither come,"
    She ofts repeats the name,
Then plunges 'neath the waters clear,
    And all is still again.

The third day comes; with eager step
    The hermit hastes to meet
The Naiad; on th' enchanted bank
    Again he takes his seat.

Soon darkness covers all the woods,
    And with returning light
Aurora comes to chase away
    The shadows of the night.

But of the hermit nought is known,
    Save that his beard was seen
By children, floating on the lake
    Two large waves between.

EXTRACT FROM A LETTER TO MRS. * * * * OF ST. LOUIS.

BUT I think I can hear you all ask what the news is,
And so, once again, I will call on the Muses.
First of all, let me tell you, New York's out of town,
We few that remain are all scorch'd and done brown,
No wonder 'tis so in this oven of bricks,
When the mercury marks in the tube ninety-six.
Now all the young ladies we mostly delight in

Have gone off to Newport,[1] or else to New Brighton,
Some are at Catskill, some at Schooley's mountain,
Some gone to Niagara, which beats the Park fountain,[2]
A number to Sharon, just now much in vogue, or
To Rockaway, Lebanon, or Saratoga.
Broadway is deserted by all of its graces,
Who are turn'd into nymphs and have sought watering places.
The glorious fourth,[3] (in some things inglorious,)

---

[1] Newport and the places afterwards mentioned are fashionable resorts in the summer season.

[2] A fountain recently erected in the Park, New York, almost rivalling those in Trafalgar Square, London.

[3] The fourth of July is the anniversary of American national independence. It is kept as a holiday throughout the Union, and in the larger towns the military volunteers parade and march through the principal streets.

Was noisy as usual and many uproarious;
The Irish on whisky became patriotic,
And perform'd many deeds which were rather Quixotic.
In rockets and fireworks not much display;
For, by some misfortune, it rain'd all the day.
And in the procession were many brave fellows,
Who shelter'd themselves from the rain with umbrellas,
Which, seeing these heroes, led me to inquire,
If they cannot stand water, how can they stand fire?
The Ravels perform every night at Niblo's,[1]
Which always is crowded, for all the world goes,
And though of the stage I have learnt much by travel,
Their wonderful tricks I can never *unravel*.

---

[1] Niblo's theatre, with its attractive garden, was at this time a favourite place of entertainment.

On dit, that there was an elopement last night
From Tenth Street; the lovers have taken to flight.
The name of the gentleman is Mr. Schott,
But that of the lady I've really forgot,
The damsel escaped through a hole in the fence,
And in my opinion she show'd her good sense,
For where's the young lady who had rather not,
If ask'd to be shot or live single, be Schott,
And now that I have written you all that here new
    is,
In return let me hear what is done in St. Louis.

ACROSTIC ADDRESSED TO SIGNORINA CLOTILDE BARILI.[1]

C hild of Italia's sunny clime,

L and of the arts, of song and rhyme,

O n thee her skies have shed the grace

T hat her old masters loved to trace.

I n Linda[2] we divide thy fears,

L augh with thy smiles, weep with thy tears;

D eceived by thine impassion'd song,

E nraged, we feel Lucia's wrong.

---

[1] Prima donna of the New York Opera House, and half sister of the celebrated Adelina Patti.

AN ACROSTIC.

B orn where the yellow Tiber flows,
A nd where the sunset softest glows,
R ome ! how much we owe to thee,
I n her another gift we see ;
L ong, long ere we the debt can pay,
I ncreasing still from day to day.

---

[2] The parts of the heroines in Donizetti's operas of Linda di Chamouni, and Lucia di Lammermoor were among the most successful ones represented by this lady.

FASHION AND PEYTONA.

What the author saw and heard on his way to, and at the great race between Fashion and Peytona, over the Long Island race-course, on the 13th May, 1845.

LL the town is going down,
    The city's moving to the races;
    Loafers, ladies, (thank God, no babies,)
Those in rags and these in laces.

At the ferry all are merry,
    Crowded, jamm'd, the steamer goes.
  "I really think the boat will sink;"
    "Some one's treading on my toes;"

"Thank God we're there;" "Sir, pay your fare;"
  "Surely we will miss the train;"
"Push on, push on;" "My purse is gone,
  D—n[1] me if I go again."

"Now we're across;" "Take care o' that horse;"
  "One dollar, nothing like the stages;"
"The man is mad;" "Here, here's my cab,
  Don't go, sir, in those railroad cages."

"Thank the stars, we're in the cars,"
  What a scene this for Annelli![2]
Such a jamming; such a cramming;
  "Lord, I'm squeezed into a jelly."

---

[1] The author begs to say that he is not responsible for the language which saluted his ears.
[2] An artist residing in New York at this time.

On, on they ride, one half outside,
    A dozen hanging on behind.
"We're in the tunnel;" "D——n that funnel,
    The smoke has almost made me blind,"

"Here's the race-course;" "Fashion's my
    horse;"
    "A hundred, sir, to seventy-five;"
"I'll take you up, sir;" "Agreed then, but, sir,
    You'll lose, as sure as I'm alive."

At every gust a cloud of dust,
    It seems that all New York is here,
Betting, joking, sweating, choking,
    Drinking wine or ginger beer.

The signal's given, they start off even,
    Fashion's warm the first mile round,

"Clear, clear the track;" "They're neck and
    neck;"
  "See Peytona's gaining ground."

Swiftly running, now they come in,
  Come in at their utmost speed;
There's now no doubt, gods! what a shout,
  The big mare has a length the lead.

At trumpet's sound, again they bound,[1]
  Each nerve Peytona strains,
"Go it, Fashion;" "Lay the lash on;"
  "Hurrah! the Southern gains!"

She beats, she beats, she wins both heats,
  Three cheers then for Peytona,

---

[1] Most races in America are run in two or three heats.

The "Southern pluck"[1] has now the luck,
I wish I were her owner.

---

[1] These contests between North and South assumed at one time an international character. The best representative of their respective stables was selected for the struggle, and from the known characteristics of the inhabitants of the two sections, the contest was said to be between " Southern pluck and Northern bottom."

A VALENTINE SENT TO MISS ✱ ✱ ✱,

LADY! do not reject in scorn a simple valentine
From one, a constant worshipper at Beauty's heavenly shrine,
Who much in foreign lands has roam'd, and seen on canvas there
Whatever the old masters traced, inspired of visions fair;
Has stood enwrapt before the walls, where Titian's colours glow'd,

And wonder'd not on such as he that kings their love bestow'd;[1]
Or where thy virgins, Raphael, in chasten'd beauty shine,
And only want the breath of God to make them all divine.
From many a form of loveliness once seen beyond the sea
Which haunts me still, from visions fair my thoughts will turn to thee.
And hear me swear, St. Valentine, whose aid this day I call,
The maid to whom these lines are sent is fairer than them all.

---

[1] The regard of the Emperor Charles V. for Titian is well known. The monarch would frequently watch the artist at his work, and, on one occasion, when the latter dropped his pencil, the Emperor raised it from the floor, and handing it to the painter, said to his astonished courtiers, "It becomes Cæsar to serve Titian."

Alas! in these degenerate times what proof can I
    e'er give
That for her sake I'd gladly die, that for her sake
    I'd live?
What monsters roam upon the earth? what dragons
    to subdue?
What mighty giants can I slay to prove my love is
    true?
Oh, had I lived in knightly days! how gladly I'd
    depart,
Your colours worn upon my breast, your image on
    my heart,
To wander forth in distant lands your beauty to
    proclaim,
And with my own good sword and shield your
    peerless charms maintain.
But these are dull prosaic times; I cannot break a
    lance,
No more knights in the lists contend, but conquer
    in the dance;

A VALENTINE.

Of old they broke fair ladies' hearts by breaking
    others' heads,
But now he wins their smiles who best the graceful
    polka treads.

Oh! had I but some little thing, some slight though
    priceless token,
A single glance to treasure up, a word of kindness
    spoken,
A faded flower, howe'er by all its wither'd charms
    despised,
Than India's richest, rarest gem, would be more
    highly prized.
Pray, when to Astor Place[1] you go, and rise to leave
    your seat,
Can you not drop by *accident* a rose-bud at your
    feet?

---

[1] An Opera-house in New York.

Which *accidentally* I'll find, and treasure up with care—
As misers guard their golden gains t'enrich some hated heir—
Reminding me in future years, should all seem dark as night,
Of one who o'er life's early path once threw a ray of light.

Lady! all happiness be yours, and smoothly down the tide
Of life, I pray, your little bark without a storm may glide;
And if one sits beside you, oh, be his love as true
As the hopeless passion this poor heart now offers up to you.

While dwells in thee, Manhattan, the maiden whom I prize,

A VALENTINE.

Sweet be the air upon thy shores, and blue above
    the skies;
And when beside thee, Hudson,[1] may thy waters
    gently flow,
And soft along the Highlands the southern zephyrs
    blow;
Or when on yonder Island, she gazes o'er the
    seas,
And stands to watch the tall, tall ships approaching
    with the breeze,
May no rude blasts assail her, that sometimes sweep
    the main,
But only soft winds kiss the cheek which I may not
    profane.

---

[1] The lady to whom these lines were addressed resided on the banks of the Hudson, passing her winters in New York and frequently visiting Staten Island, which commands a beautiful view of the harbour of the "Empire City" and its approaches from the ocean.

CORALIE.

A SKETCH.

IN a Square, at number three,
Lives the fair Miss Coralie.
If you roam from France to China,
You'll not meet a girl that's finer.
Every city you may seek in,
London, Paris, New York, Pekin,
None such varied charms display,
Mortal, goddess, nymph, or fée.
She is often call'd divine,

One of the Three, one of the Nine.
In accomplishments excels,
And she is the belle of belles;
Of all languages is master,
And in singing rivals Pasta,
But she goes an octave higher,
And in playing beats De Meyer;
Sketches too, and draws, and paints
Heads of warriors and of saints,
Rattles French off, with a flow
Of language, quite unknown at Bow;[1]
Speaks Italian, and talks Spanish
With an accent Catalanish,
German, Arabic, Chinese,
Patagonian, Japanese,
Then she polks so light and airy,
You would think it was a fairy

---

[1] *Vide* Chaucer's Canterbury Tales.

CORALIE.

Whom you held around the waist.
Would you like to know her taste?
She's connoisseur in all the arts,
And delights in golden hearts,
Love's sugar-candy, wedding cake,
And at midnight to awake,
Listening to a serenade;
Likes a puzzle or charade,
Famous for her skill in tricks,
(Some of them surpass old Nick's),
And she measures five feet six.

She's had lovers of all ages,
Names enough to fill six pages;
I would write them down, but think
I have not sufficient ink.
This I'll say, and 'tis no boast,
They outnumber'd Pharaoh's host.
She has been admired, adored

By natives of all lands explored;
Spanish Dons and Counts from Prussia,
Baron Kickusoff of Russia,
Yangfum Kewang Yihae Tonkin,
A famous three tail'd Mandarin,
A Pawnee chief, fresh from Nebraska,
And Prince Taboo of Madagascar.

Young man, whoe'er you are, beware,
And look not on this lady fair,
'Twere better far for me or you, sir,
To gaze upon that wretch, Medusa;
I'd rather be a petrifaction
Than be driven to distraction;
Better face an alligator,
She is such a captivator.

She's had no end of declarations
From lovers of all ranks and nations,

And sent replies, each one refusing,
Which these poor devils on perusing,
(I judge so from the way they acted,)
Their senses lost and went distracted.
Some of them for Texas started,
And others died quite broken-hearted;
Some in Hudson's stream were drown'd,
And some preferr'd Long Island Sound;
Some chose a pistol, some a sword,
Some hung themselves up by a cord,
And kick'd until their necks were broken,
And some fought duels at Hoboken,[1]
All efforts vain to reconcile 'em.
Some in a lunatic asylum,

---

[2] Hoboken, in the State of New Jersey, and on the side of the Hudson opposite to New York, was the favourite resort of the hot bloods of the latter place for settling "affairs of honour."

In spite of padding and strait jacket,
Keep up a most confounded racket;
And to that place, if my friends knew
That I wrote this, they'd send me too.

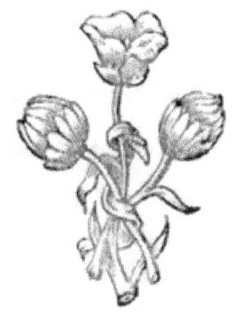

AN ACROSTIC TO A YOUNG LADY OF PHILADELPHIA.

A mid the groves where Schuylkill flows,
N ow with a gentle motion,
N ow rushes wildly 'tween its banks,
A nd seeks the distant ocean,

L ives there a maid as wondrous fair
A s she of Susquehannah,
M ourn'd o'er by Campbell's classic muse,
B efore there lived an Anna.

LINES ON THE FANCY BALL,

GIVEN AT THE OCEAN HOUSE IN NEWPORT, RHODE ISLAND, ON THE 19TH OF AUGUST 1846, SENT TO MISS * * * WHO APPEARED THERE IN THE CHARACTER OF FENELLA.

AT evening, in my rocking chair
    I swing with gentle motion,
    While Fancy paints the fancy ball
In Newport, at the Ocean.

In spite of politics or Polk,[1]
    Of Clay, of corn, or cotton,

---

[1] Polk and Clay, rival candidates for the Presidency.

That night will be remember'd long,
    That scene be unforgotten.

Here's every costume since the time
    Of Egypt and the Pharaohs,
Crusaders, courtiers and clowns,
    And Spanish caleseros.[1]

The savage Indian smiles and bows,
    And looks extremely pleasant;
The haughty prince forgets his rank,
    And dances with a peasant.

Russians and Poles walk arm in arm,
    And Turks take wine together,

---

[1] Pronounced calaysayro. The driver of an open carriage in Spain, called calesa. The author's costume on this occasion.

And Ravenswood[1] is very gay,
　In cap without the feather.

A pale faced nun all robed in white,
　Is waltzing with a templar;
That monk who near the table stands,
　Must be a bad exemplar.

A knight approaches to confess,
　With holy resolution,
The monk first gives a glass of wine;
　Then gives him absolution.

Hopes he may slay a thousand Turks,
　When next he makes a campaign,

---

[1] After the Master of Ravenswood had disappeared in the quicksand the only trace of him found by his faithful Caleb, who hurried towards the spot, was the sable feather of his cap which the rising tide washed to his old follower's feet.

The penance I can't think sincere,
  Because 'tis nought but *champagne*.

Rebecca takes a slice of ham,
  Of Jewish laws a breaker;
The novice too forgets her vows,
  While flirting with a Quaker.

In spite of glass, no lady here
  Polks more than Cinderella;
In spite of tongue, no lady fair
  Talks more than mute Fenella.

The African is carrying out
  His views of " 'malgamation,"
The marquis with the milkmaid chats,
  Unmindful of his station.

Where are they all? Newport, alas!
  Is now almost deserted,

The beaux have fled who flourish'd there;
    The belles with whom they flirted.

Some have gone home to dream of stocks,
    And some of sweet Fenella,
And some have left a heart behind,
    And some—a silk umbrella.

Some boldly brave the Atlantic wave
    In steamship or in "liner,"[1]
And some are on their way to bed;
    Some—on their way to China.

And some are dashing through Broadway,
    Between a horse and tiger;
Some seek a Paris sauce, and some
    The sources of the Niger;

---

[1] The packet ships or "liners," plying at this time between New York and Liverpool, London and Havre, were unrivalled for speed and comfort.

A FANCY BALL.

And some are making fortunes now,
    And some are making purses,
And some are writing learned briefs,
    Some writing silly verses.

I'm seated in my rocking chair,
    While Fancy softly traces,
Like morning dreams, the Newport scenes
    And Newport's pleasant faces.

Whatever clime, in after time,
    The Fates may cast my lot in,
One scene will be remember'd long,
    One face be unforgotten.

New York, *Sept.* 15*th*, 1846.

A VOICE FROM CALIFORNIA.

Written on the news reaching England that the State of California had adopted a Constitution prohibiting Slavery in her territory. While the Author's views in regard to this institution remain unchanged, riper years have taught him to look more charitably upon those who differ from him in opinion.

 VOICE from California
    Is borne across the sea;
It brings the joyful tidings
    That land of gold is free.

And since to me, o'er ocean,
    The happy message came,
With firmer step and prouder,
    I boast my country's name.

A VOICE FROM CALIFORNIA.

Where Sacramento's waters
    In golden channels flow,
And where the proud Sierras
    Lift high their heads of snow,

Where herds of untamed horses
    Sweep over boundless plains,
Shall rise no groans from bondsmen,
    No sounds of clanking chains.

Free as her desert chargers,
    She comes to join us now,
And pure as are the snowflakes
    That crown Nevada's brow.

The sacred cause of freedom
    Henceforth unites our fate,
Then hail with fondest welcome,
    Our youngest sister State.

Then forward, fellow soldiers,
    The holy strife's begun;
We must not sheathe our weapons
    Because one battle's won.

By fire-side, bar, and pulpit,
    Still plead for Freedom's cause,
And freely, boldly, use the means
    Within our country's laws.

The God of battles with us,
    We'll fight throughout the land,
And like to him of Naseby,
    The Bible in our hand;

Though sophists from its pages
    The blackest lies may tell,
And dare to brand their Maker
    With deeds that come from hell.

A VOICE FROM CALIFORNIA.

The coward priest who falters
   In battling for the right,
Must one day hear the question,
   "What, watchman, of the night?"

What though the politician
   Refuse to share our toils,
He does not love his country,
   But loves that country's spoils.

And if *Virginia's chivalry*
   Affect a proud disdain,
The curse of God is on him
   Who feels not slavery's stain.

But like to our forefathers,
   Who freed us with the sword,
Each man within his conscience
   Will find a full reward.

And so in distant ages,
   Some future bard may rise
And sing of those who conquer'd
   The Devil and his lies;

And eloquence, all glowing,
   Will make the warm blood boil,
In telling of the men who won
   The freedom of the soil.

LINES ADDRESSED TO MISS * * *, OF KATONAH, NEW YORK,

SHORTLY AFTER THE AUTHOR'S RETURN TO LONDON FROM THE UNITED STATES; IN IMITATION OF A POPULAR ENGLISH POET.

 CITY, dim and vast,
Meets my bewilder'd gaze;
A cloud of smoke o'erhead
Shuts out the solar rays;
The streets are swept and clean;[1]

---

[1] Every traveller coming to London from New York is impressed on his arrival in the British metropolis by the sombre appearance of the houses and cleanliness of the streets.

The houses dingy brown;
Can you be at Katonah,
And I in London town?

Lord Farintosh goes by,
Driven in gorgeous state;
His coachman's legs in silk,
And white wig on his pate;
Behind, two footmen tall
Put on a stately frown;
Yes, yes, you're at Katonah,
And I'm in London town.

The cabs which rush about,
Or stand upon the " rank;"
The " 'busses" red which ply
From Hammersmith to Bank;
The statues of the Duke,

LINES.

(I wish they'd take them down,)
Proclaim you're at Katonah,
And I'm in London town.

These shops for "Alton ale
And sandwiches for lunch;"
The "heavy swells" I meet,
Just like you've seen in *Punch;*
And those three well-known youths,
Jones, Robinson, and Brown,
Declare you're at Katonah,
While I'm in London town.

This boy, who for a copper
Will stand upon his head,
Unless he see approaching
Policeman X Y Z:
The shop signs "by appointment,"

With unicorn and crown,
Tell me you're at Katonah,
And I'm in London town.

The drive within the Park,
Where rank and fashion go ;
The splendid thoroughbreds
That dash through Rotten Row;
This placid Serpentine,
Where one may skate or drown,
All say you're at Katonah,
While I'm in London town.

And thus am I reminded
By something, every day,
That I am here in England,
While you are far away ;

And though our girls are pretty
As ever wore a gown,
My heart is at Katonah,
Though I'm in London town.

www.ingramcontent.com/pod-product-compliance
Lightning Source LLC
Chambersburg PA
CBHW020243090426
42735CB00010B/1812